MOODS OF THE

LAKELAND FELLS

JON SPARKS

HALSGROVE

First published in Great Britain in 2006

British Library Cataloguing-in-Publication Data
A CIP record for this title is available from the British Library

ISBN 1 84114 526 2
ISBN 978 1 84114 526 6

HALSGROVE
Halsgrove House
Lower Moor Way
Tiverton, Devon EX16 6SS
Tel: 01884 243242
Fax: 01884 243325
email: sales@halsgrove.com
website: www.halsgrove.com

Printed and bound by D'Auria Industrie Grafiche Spa, Italy

INTRODUCTION

Compiling a book like this is a curious process. It involves sifting through hundreds or thousands of images, gradually whittling them down to a short list, and then to the final selection. Then the images have to be given some sort of order, and finally I have to go through them one-by-one to write the captions.

In doing this with these images of the Lakeland Fells, I have had a powerful reminder of how much the fells have meant to me, and the enormous variety of experience they have given me. Much is in the eye of the beholder, and I have approached the fells as a walker, climber, scrambler and mountain-biker, as well as a photographer. But variety also resides in the fells themselves.

Just how do the Lakeland Fells manage to present such diversity of moods and aspects? They have no volcanoes nor glaciers, they are not very high, and the whole area is quite compact. From any high Lakeland summit (given decent visibility), the view reaches beyond the district itself, perhaps to the quite different upland landscape of the north Pennines, the glistening sands of Morecambe Bay or the waters of the Irish Sea. On really clear days the Isle of Man, Scotland and – more rarely – Wales are all in view.

To me the scale of the place is part of its charm: not so big that the fells are out of reach, nor so small that they merge into the lowlands. Even a half-day walk can take you from lush valleys to bare summits, so variety is inbuilt.

Diversity also comes from a rich and complex geology. Within the broad divisions that I learned in school – Skiddaw Slates, Borrowdale Volcanics, and so on – there are enormous local variations. The underlying rock affects not just the landforms, but soil and vegetation. It has also provided rich pickings for miners and quarrymen.

The weather also helps. The district's rainy reputation is often overplayed. Again the key word is variety. Whatever else it is, it's rarely boring. On 'bad' days in particular, I keep in mind John Ruskin's words:

> *Sunshine is delicious, rain is refreshing, wind braces us up, snow is exhilarating; There is really no such thing as bad weather, only different kinds of good weather.*

This sentiment might sound hollow in Antarctica, or in the drought-stricken regions of Africa, but in the Lakes it carries conviction. Here, the elements rarely make you fear for your life – given proper equipment and experience. Nor are the fells too big, or too steep, to be enjoyed in virtually any conditions.

Still, some days, and conditions, are undeniably better than others. To me, winter is the prime season. Snow, frost and ice have the power to transform the landscape, and the low winter sun means that the light can be magical all day long. I must confess I also appreciate being able to catch a sunset and still get to the pub in good time!

Spring and summer excite me less, at least for pure landscape photography. There's too much green, and warmer weather also increases the temptation of other pursuits like climbing and mountain biking. In fact many of my best summer shots have been taken after a day's climbing, and several appear in this book.

As summer tilts into autumn, the fells become more colourful. It starts with the heather in August, but it's when the bracken turns orange in October that the palette really begins to liven up. Around this time we also usually get the first frosts, and a greater chance of really crystal-clear visibility. And so the year slips once again into winter, when good thermals, warm gloves and a head-torch are all essential items of photographic kit.

So a high proportion of the photographs in this book are from autumn and winter, but every season – and every month – is represented. What you won't find is every single fell. There are already several books which catalogue the fells admirably. What I have tried to capture is the range of light and shade, colour and shape, the ever-changing weather, the myriad ways that people work and play on the fells; in a word, their moods.

Jon Sparks, April 2006

Lake District National Park

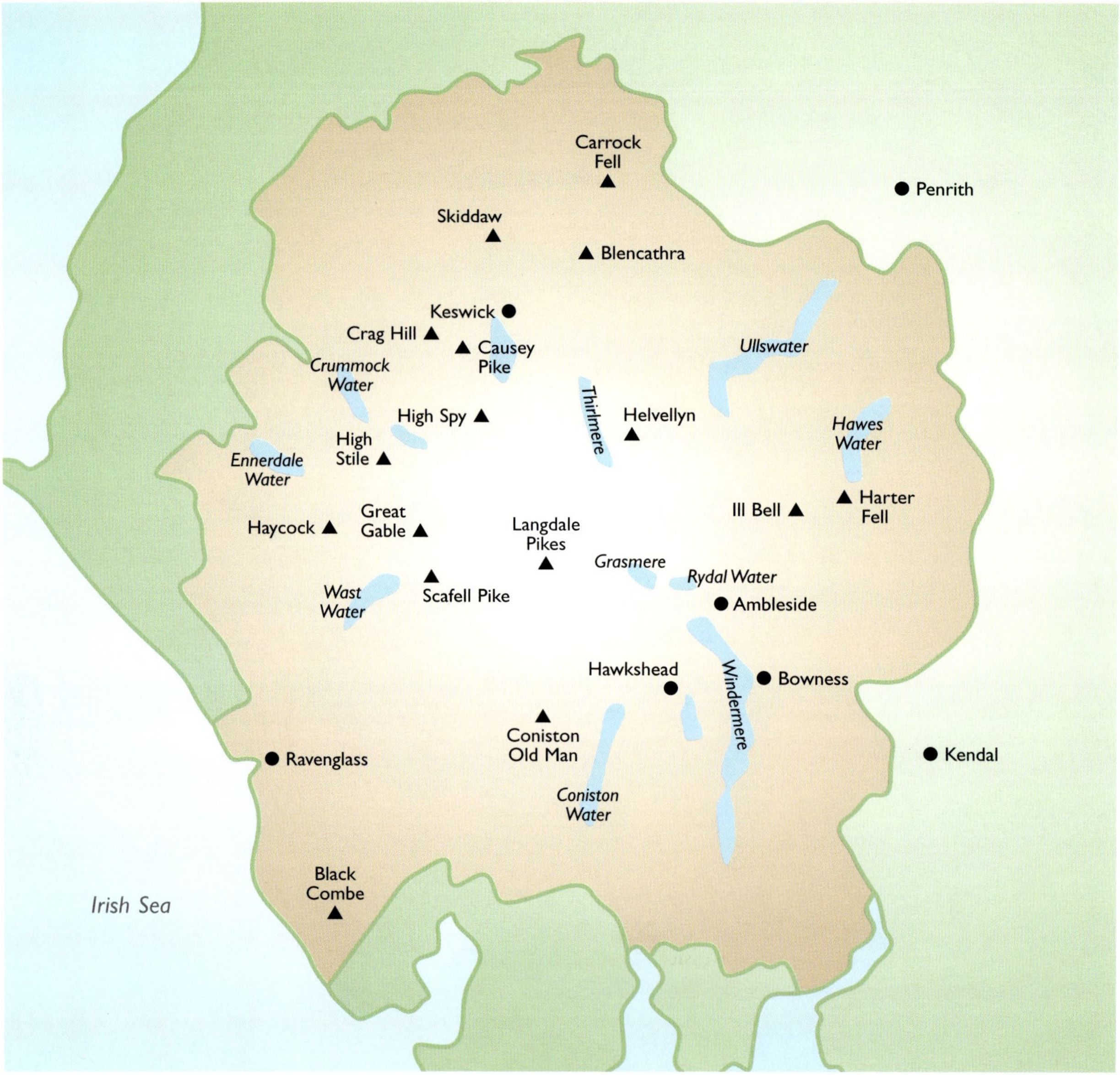

Ice crystals on cairn, Stybarrow Dodd
It takes very specific conditions to form crystals like these: freezing fog and a steady wind. However, it was a lot easier to appreciate their beauty on a calm, sunny day.

Mosedale

Mosedale, which just means 'marshy valley', is also a common name, and this one is probably the best-known. It lies just north of Wasdale Head. The fell at the head of the valley is Pillar.

Opposite: **Sour Milk Gill, Easedale, looking towards Grasmere**

Many placenames recur across the Lake District, a reminder of the times when the dales were far more isolated than they are today. Simple descriptive names like Raven Crag are common, but the more poetic inspiration of Sour Milk Gill is also repeated several times, with well-known examples in Borrowdale and Buttermere as well as Easedale.

The Coniston Fells from Selside – winter

Opposite: **The Coniston Fells from Selside – summer**

Much of the low fell country east of Coniston Water is blanketed by the conifers of Grizedale Forest, but there is also a broad swathe of open moor, reaching its highest point at Top o'Selside. The views from this area over the lake to the Coniston Fells are some of the finest in the Lake District. These two shots are taken from similar, though not identical, positions, overlooking the deserted farmhouse of Low Parkamoor.

Ripples, Swindale

Rocks and water are two of the the primary elements of the landscape, especially in the Lake District.
I could happily spend whole days photographing nothing else.

Shadows, Crag Hill
Crag Hill (also known as Eel Crag) is one of the main tops in the north-western fells. On this wonderful winter day, visibility extended far into Scotland: those are the Galloway Hills on the horizon.

Castlerigg Stone Circle and Helvellyn

There are many theories about stone circles like Castlerigg, but we can never know for certain exactly what motivated their builders to such efforts. However, it's hard to believe that they were not at least partly inspired by the location, overlooked by the fells we now call Skiddaw, Blencathra and Helvellyn.

Cairn on Harter Fell

Harter Fell is another recurring name; this is the eastern one, above the valleys of Kentmere, Mardale and Longsleddale. The fell in the background, left of the cairn, is High Street.

Evening light over Torver High Common

I found it difficult to put a short title to this picture, which was taken as we were walking out after a long day climbing on Dow Crag. Torver High Common is merely one area in the middle distance. The hollow in the foreground is known as The Cove, and the view also extends over the Blawith Fells. Morecambe Bay is just discernible in the distance, while Coniston Water can be glimpsed at the left of the picture.

Rainbow over Rydal, with Fairfield behind
Everybody loves rainbows; the problem is that a big showy rainbow tends to dominate everything in the picture. I rather liked this more modest, and short-lived, display.

Pillar Rock from High Stile

Pillar Rock gives its name to the fell, rather than the other way around, as is more usual. The aptness of the name is well illustrated in this long-lens view from High Stile, in the light of a high summer evening. Two lucky climbers can just be seen high on the face; I'm fairly certain they are on the route known as the New West, one of the finest 'easy' climbs in the Lakes.

Cornice, Helvellyn

This is the sight that greeted me at the top of a winter climb on Helvellyn's Brown Cove Crags. After a couple of hours in the blue shadows, the sunlight on the sculpted snow was quite magical. I wasn't sure how long it would last and I took the photograph even before I turned my attention to establishing a belay.

Herdwick sheep on the slopes of Buckbarrow

Stocky and tough, the Herdwick is the quintessential local breed of sheep on the Lakeland Fells.

Looking towards Harter Fell

Again, this is the eastern Harter Fell (see also p13). However, I wasn't really interested in making a portrait of the hill; I was much more concerned with the narrow palette of colours that this view presented, as if the haze was filtering out certain hues.

Sprinkling Tarn and Great End
There could hardly be a more prosaic-sounding name than Great End, and yet it is poetic in its aptness. Here the high ridge running north from Scafell Pike is abruptly terminated; dropping a full 300 metres to Sprinkling Tarn, a nice name, but much less blunt.

Opposite: **Walker approaching Grisedale Pike**
At first glance this shot may give a deceptive impression of warmth. In fact, though there was barely any snow on the fells, it was bitterly cold.

Walker on Crinkle Crags

The terrain on Crinkle Crags is as complex as the name suggests, and it's potentially confusing even in clear weather. In mist it requires careful navigation.

Scandale and the head of Windermere

Afters several hours walking in the clouds, we dropped below them at Scandale Pass and enjoyed this view down the valley towards Ambleside and Windermere. The smaller body of water beyond is Blelham Tarn.

Catstycam and Helvellyn
The pyramidal peak of Catstycam stands out well from this angle, but it is really only a satellite peak of Helvellyn, whose summit is directly in line with the sun.

Opposite: **Great Langdale and the Langdale Pikes**
The Langdale Pikes are easily recognisable from a wide range of angles. To my mind, one of the best areas for viewing them is on the low ridge between Langdale and Grasmere, and I've made several visits here looking for the best viewpoint. On this day I was lucky with the dramatic break in the clouds. The lack of foreground interest didn't seem to matter.

Wood anemones, Ill Crag
We came across these anemones quite unexpectedly in the upper reaches of Eskdale, on the scrambling route on Ill Crag – and a long way from any woods.

Path below Causey Pike
I was initially attracted by the strong light on the rocks and bracken but, with the shadowy peak beyond, this shot also seems to me to evoke the sense of anticipation at the start of a day on the fells.

Cairn on Brown Pike
Brown Pike is a minor rise on the ridge leading to Dow Crag and is the first, or last, top of the day for many walkers on the Coniston Fells. Even after the sun disappeared into the haze over the Irish Sea, we lingered a while in the softer light.

Opposite: **Evening, slopes of Helvellyn**
The scalloped form of this hollow in the snow, a chance result of sun and wind, irresistibly reminded me of a seashell. I tried to balance it with the distant peaks, which include Scafell Pike and Great Gable.

Lichen-covered rock, Bowscale Tarn
I'd gone to photograph the tarn for an earlier book in this series, but was equally inspired by this nearby rock.

Scoat Fell from Haycock

Drystone walls are a familiar feature on the lower slopes of most fells, but there are relatively few places where they extend right across the tops. This is probably the most striking example of all, extending for several kilometres further west beyond Haycock.

Summit of Bowscale Fell
This circular shelter stands right at the summit of Bowscale Fell. I really wished for a wider angled lens to get it all in. The peak in the background, seen from a relatively unfamiliar angle, is Blencathra.

Little Stand and the Scafell range

Little Stand will probably be an unfamiliar name to many walkers – it doesn't, for instance, figure on the list of 'Wainwrights' – and yet it is a fell of respectable height with a definite summit. The ridge continues to Crinkle Crags.

Cairn, Harper Hills
Harper Hills is a very minor bump on the rolling fells a few miles west of Shap, but someone has taken the trouble to honour it with a cairn. On the skyline are High Street, Kidsty Pike and High Raise.

Walkers in the Glenderamackin valley

The River Glenderamackin runs below the east side of Blencathra, one of its main feeders being Scales Tarn.

Greenburn and Great Carrs

Greenburn is another of those names which occurs more than once; there's one near Grasmere, but this is the better-known one in the Coniston Fells, overlooked by Wetherlam, Swirl How and Great Carrs. Most walkers follow the flanking ridges and the valley is relatively unfrequented, but it's a rewarding place to explore, with an old mine, a tarn, and some attractive cascades.

Opposite: **Evening on Grey Knotts**

Grey Knotts has a broad hummocky summit area with a number of pools, making it a good place to linger on a fine evening. I took shots in various directions, including this one towards Helvellyn.

Smithy Beck and Buckbarrow

Buckbarrow is more of a facade than a real peak; behind the crags the ridge rises gently to Seatallan. However from this angle it's impressive enough, and the crags are popular with climbers.

Opposite: **Catbells and Skiddaw**

It's 'Cat Bells' (two words) on the Ordnance Survey maps, but one word on Harvey's. Take your pick. Either way, it's one of the best-loved fells. The climb is steep but short and the narrow ridge gives grand views, especially of Skiddaw, in the background.

Blencathra from the Castlerigg Stone Circle
A momentary break in the clouds threw vivid light on the lower slopes of Blease Fell, which is the western shoulder of Blencathra. The apparent summit in the middle is the top of Gategill Fell while the main summit (Hallsfell Top) is the one further back.

Opposite: **Sunset over Ennerdale, Haystacks and High Stile**
There may be no bad days to be on the fells, but some are better than others and a few – like this one – are very special. We'd climbed some fine routes on Gable Crag, finishing with the fabulous Engineer's Slabs, before walking out along the ancient track of Moses' Trod. The streamers of cloud spilling from the Buttermere valley into Ennerdale turned a beautiful sunset into something quite extraordinary.

Knowe Crags, Blencathra

Knowe Crags fringe the top of Blease Fell at the west end of the ridge of Blencathra. The fell on the right is Crag Hill and the Irish Sea gleams in the far distance.

Descending from Froswick
After a fine walk over Yoke, Ill Bell and Froswick, we dropped back down towards the Troutbeck valley in the last light of the sun. Windermere lies in the shadows in the distance.

The Napes crags, Great Gable

The Napes crags on the south face of Great Gable have a special place in the history of British rock-climbing. The famous Napes Needle (first climbed in 1886) stands at the base of Needle Ridge, just right of the right-hand gully. The central mass is known as Eagle's Nest Ridge and to its left is the smaller Arrowhead Ridge.

Rocks on Dow Crag
These spiky rocks are quite typical of Dow Crag and the Coniston Fells, but this outcrop stood out particularly well against a shadowy backdrop.

Whiteside col

Snow sweeping across the ground and around the feet of the walkers gives a clue that it was blowing a near gale. This meant that the clouds were occasionally shredded to reveal glimpses of sunlit fells beyond.

Christmas on the rocks, Bowfell
It was slow going across the summit of Bowfell, with deep drifts of snow between the tumbled rocks, but I thought it was worth the effort. Incidentally, it happened to be Christmas Day.

Highford Beck

Highford Beck is on Birker Fell, between Eskdale and the Duddon valley. I'd hoped for a few breaks in the cloud during the day but had very little joy; however, when big views are impossible there are always miniature landscapes to look at. And I did get lucky right at the end of the day (see p 80).

Ice, Crinkle Gill
This was just the beginning of a cold spell, and the ice formations were still very fragile.

Scandale

This shot was taken from a very similar spot to the one on p23, but under rather more benign conditions.

Cascades, Dungeon Ghyll
Dungeon Ghyll is a very well-known name but only those who are prepared to scramble, and possibly get quite wet, will see this lovely cascade.

Pike o'Stickle

Pike o'Stickle is the westernmost top of the Langdale Pikes. The conspicuous pale scree-gully on its right is well known as the site of a Neolithic stone axe 'factory'.

Troughton Beck
Troughton Beck is just west of Pike o'Stickle, and for anyone who doesn't mind a little gentle scrambling, it offers a most attractive and remarkably quiet route to the tops. The peaks on the skyline are Crinkle Crags and Bowfell.

Miton Hill, Carrock Fell

The biggest challenge in taking this shot was keeping the camera steady in a buffeting gale. Even if I'd had a tripod with me it might not have helped, and I don't think my companions would have tolerated the delay.

Cairn on White Maiden

White Maiden is a relatively little-known outlier of the Coniston Fells, but it has a lovely summit with excellent views. Here, Scafell and Scafell Pike lurk in the clouds while Esk Pike stands out as a distinctive peak; to its right Bowfell and Crinkle Crags appear almost as one.

Wall on Shipman Knotts
When not regularly maintained, drystone walls don't so much collapse as slowly subside. The distant hills are Coniston Old Man and Wetherlam.

Opposite: **Blencathra**
This is a good angle from which to see how Blencathra got its alternative, uglier, but undoubtedly descriptive name of Saddleback.

Herdwick sheep, Dow Bank

These Herdwicks seemed happy enough in the winter sunshine: I had the distinct impression they were smiling for the camera.

Rushes, above Swindale
Rushes are a familiar sight over most of the fell country, especially in the damper places.

Ice detail, Glade How
I originally planned to use this pool as a bit of foreground interest for a general landscape shot, but then I took a closer look and forgot all about the broader view.

Calf Hole and Ruthwaite Cove

The word 'cove' is widely used in the Lake District as an equivalent to the Scottish 'corrie' or Welsh 'cwm'. There is a string of combes along the eastern side of the Helvellyn range: Calf Hole is part of Nethermost Cove; the sunlit ridge separates it from Ruthwaite Cove. (There's a face-on view on page 95.)

Rock detail, Brant Fell
Brant Fell is a low hill just outside Bowness-on-Windermere, with the winning combination of easy access and excellent views. It also boasts some little slate outcrops just below the summit. Some of them are steep enough to provide small-scale climbing practice, though its popularity has declined somewhat following the development of indoor climbing walls.

Westmorland's Route, Dove Crag
This is about as far from an indoor climbing wall as you can get in the Lake District. Though technically easy, the route is long and complex, with some loose rock and some very exposed sections. Far below are the Hartsop valley and a corner of Brothers Water.

Map lichen

Map lichen (*Rhizocarpon geographicum*), which forms the yellow patches here, is so perfectly named that I felt the flat surface and relatively flat light in this shot were wholly appropriate.

Sheepfold below Glade How

Sheepfolds are a common sight in the fells but few are as elaborate or as beautiful as this one. I thought initially I should take a closer look but realised that the layout showed up more clearly from a distance. The fact that it saved me a detour was immaterial, of course.

Wetherlam from Tarn Hows Intake

I have a soft spot for Wetherlam. It's not one of the most glamorous fells, but there's a lot of interest on and around its extensive slopes. It's also visible from my back garden about 40km away, though I prefer to photograph it from closer range.

Descending from Wetherlam

Wetherlam is a big complex fell, with several ridges and valleys. This is the descent into Red Dell. Coniston Water lies below, and Morecambe Bay is in the far distance.

Temperature inversion, from Haycock

Every now and then you set out on a day that doesn't look too promising, and it ends up like this, with cloud over the lowlands while the high fells are bathed in sunshine. The nearest slopes are the flanks of Seatallan, linked to Middle Fell; an edge of Greendale Tarn can be seen. The intermediate ridge is Whin Rigg and in the distance are Whit Fell and Black Combe.
I subsequently learned that in Lancaster and Preston it stayed murky all day.

Clouds over Bowscale Fell
The forecast was anything but encouraging, but we began the ascent of Carrock Fell in warm sunshine (p76). The clouds rolled in soon enough, but before they closed in they treated us to some gorgeous light effects.

Clouds over Wetherlam

Days like this, when thick cloud alternates with bright sunshine and the light changes by the second, make landscape photography a pretty dynamic business; you might not need quite the razor-sharp reflexes of the sports photographer, but you do need to stay alert.

Rocks on Erin Crag

Part of the charm of the Lake District is its complex geology; the variety of colours and textures in the rock is never-ending. And there's probably nowhere better to appreciate this than the Coniston Fells.

Esk Buttress and Scafell Pike

Scafell Pike is England's highest mountain, and this is its finest aspect, overlooking the wild spaces of Upper Eskdale. The crag in the centre is marked on some maps as Dow Crag but climbers call it Esk Buttress to avoid any confusion with 'the' Dow Crag above Coniston. It has some magnificent rock climbs, including the awesome Central Pillar, which is one of the best routes I have ever done.

The Pudding Stone

There are quite a few individually named boulders around the District. Borrowdale's Bowder Stone is the best known and next must surely be the Pudding Stone, in Boulder Valley above Coniston. Climbers have made a dozen or so routes to its top, the easiest being the ramps facing the camera.

Ascending Helvellyn

As we neared the ridge after the long pull up from Wythburn we knew this was going to be something special: days like this don't come along very often. Several winters might go by without ever seeing the unbeatable combination of good snow cover, no wind, a cloudless sky and fantastic visibility.

Cotton-grass, Bell Crags

Cotton grass is also known as bog cotton, which gives a useful clue as to where you'll find it; its white tufts are a good indicator of places where it is probably too wet to walk.

Ascending Carrock Fell

I put on a spurt to get ahead so I could photograph my companions coming up; when I turned to take this shot I realised that the clouds were rolling towards Bowscale Fell. It wasn't very long after this that I got the shot seen on p69.

Opposite: **Sheep on Brown Pike, evening**

Rock-climbing can mean long days and as Dow Crag is one of my favourite places to climb, I've often found myself walking down over Brown Pike in the late evening, though it's never looked better than this. Harter Fell is on the left of the picture, with Scafell and Scafell Pike on the right.

Crummock Water and Loweswater

This shot was taken from Whiteless Pike, in the early stages of a memorable day on the north-western fells. There was no wind to disturb the calm of Crummock Water, which perfectly reflected the ridge of Mellbreak. The smaller lake is Loweswater and beyond that are the Solway Firth and Galloway.

Walkers on Walna Scar

The Walna Scar 'road' (really a rough track much abused by off-road vehicles) is a familiar approach to the Coniston Fells, but relatively few walkers venture south from it over Walna Scar itself to White Maiden and White Pike. Apart from its intrinsic attractions, this walk gives an unfamiliar perspective on the higher fells; that's the summit of Dow Crag on the left and Buck Pike on the right.

Ancient cairn below Rough Crag

The Birker Fell area, west of the Duddon valley, has a number of ancient remains, including this cairn. It would have been close to impossible to secure this shot on film, because of the extreme difference in brightness between the foreground and the background. With a digital camera on a tripod, it was possible to take several shots, identically framed but with widely differing exposures, to record detail both in the cairn and in the sky. It still took quite a bit of work on the computer to blend them together.

Bubbles under ice, High Goat Gill
Ice and sunlight were the themes of the day, and I was looking for a shot that said something about them. The regularity of these trapped bubbles seemed to sum it up perfectly.

South cairn, Haycock
This shot is taken from the same position as the one on p68, and only a few minutes earlier. Although it was January and the ground was frozen, the air was so still and the sun so warm that I was comfortable wearing just a T-shirt and trousers for most of the day.

Opposite: **The valley of Sail Beck**
Not every fell-walk has to go to a summit. A fine example is the route through the north-western fells by way of Sail Beck and Rigg Beck, which in its way is just as dramatic and often a lot less busy than the containing ridges. The pass between the two valleys frames a view of Causey Pike.

Black Combe

Black Combe just fails to make 2000 feet in old money, and therefore doesn't quite qualify as a mountain (by the most popular definition). But this is no reason to neglect this fine fell, which has the best sea views of any English hill. Wordsworth claimed for it 'the widest uninterrupted prospect that English ground commands', and I see no reason to disagree. It also has one of the most evenly graded ascents of any major hill, and as it's a bridleway one of my ambitions is to take my mountain bike up – and down.

Glenderaterra Beck and Great Calva

Glenderaterra Beck runs down the dramatic gap between Skiddaw and Blencathra and offers easy routes through to the rolling, lonely hills 'Back o'Skidda'. The symmetrical form of Great Calva stands in line with the gap.

Wall above Naddle Beck

There's a Naddle Beck near Keswick but this is the one further east, near Shap. I liked the banded effect created by the wall and shadows, but it didn't quite make a picture until I found this tree to break up the overwhelming horizontals.

Opposite: **Summit of Swirl How**

Although Coniston Old Man is a metre or so higher, Swirl How is the meeting place of the main ridges of the Coniston Fells. The Old Man has great views over the lower country of southern Lakeland – lovely in its own way – while Swirl How is a better place for mountain views like this one, to Scafell, Scafell Pike, Bowfell and Crinkle Crags.

Wastwater, approaching snowstorm
Not long before this shot was taken, we'd climbed Napes Needle in warm sunshine. Seconds after the shot was taken, we were engulfed in a near-blizzard. It didn't last very long and an hour or so later we climbed Needle Ridge on rock that was once again dry.

Opposite: **Skiddaw and Blencathra from High Stile**
We'd spent the night on the summit of High Stile, and this was our reward. By the time the first 'day' walkers reached the top, the mist had all but gone and the light was considerably flatter – though still attractive.

Walkers on Wandope
Wandope (sometimes called Wanlope) is an outlier of Grasmoor in the north-western fells.

Opposite: **Icy cairn, Stybarrow Dodd**
I crouched low to help the cairn stand out against the winter sky. Helvellyn is on the extreme left of the shot; the more distinct peak is Helvellyn Lower Man. To the right of the cairn are Esk Pike and Scafell Pike.

Striding Edge and St Sunday Crag
On such a perfect winter day it's hardly surprising that there were many people out enjoying themselves. There are over two dozen people on Striding Edge in this photo and several hundred must have visited the top of Helvellyn during the day.

Opposite: **Coniston Fells from Hawkshead Hill**
Though the early morning light gives a feeling of warmth, it was bitterly cold on this January morning.

Helvellyn from Kidsty Pike
Cloud-shadows help to separate the various ridges in this view. Helvellyn is on the left, with the pointed peak of Catstycam near the centre and White Side and Raise further right.

Opposite: **Dollywaggon Pike and Nethermost Pike**
This shot was taken near Lanty's Tarn, above Glenridding, and gives a fair impression of the glacial sculpting of the eastern side of the Helvellyn range.

Rock detail, Easedale

This rock had obviously been fractured very recently as some of the surfaces were completely fresh and unweathered. I liked the contrast between these and the lichen-covered face. Despite the strikingly-straight lines, it's all completely natural.

Striding Edge and Helvellyn
Striding Edge is the best-known and most sought-after of Lakeland's aretes (narrow ridges). In good conditions it's little more than a walk: there are only one or two places which call for hands to be used. However, it shouldn't be underestimated: in icy conditions, or high winds, it can be a lot more demanding.

Above Tarn Crag

Tarn Crag lies just below Stickle Tarn, on the most popular route to the Langdale Pikes, and offers a few pleasant easy climbs and scrambles. Above the main crag are many small outcrops of wonderfully rough rock.

Opposite: **Cascade, Troughton Beck**

Troughton Beck is full of little cascades and waterfalls. It's best suited to a leisurely ascent, and for the photographer it can take a very long time.

Bowfell

The viewpoint for this shot is not too far from that on p25, though lower down, and it's obviously taken in a different season. The shadowy shoulder in the middle distance is part of Lingmoor Fell.

Walkers on Nethermost Pike

I was very grateful to these two walkers; not only did they appear in just the right place at the right time, but they were both wearing red. I couldn't have arranged it better if I'd set the whole thing up.

Robinson

I've heard people say that there can't possibly be a hill just called Robinson; it has to be Robinson Fell or Robinson Pike. But all the maps agree; plain Robinson it is.

Derwent Water from Skiddaw

Strictly speaking the viewpoint is not Skiddaw itself but Skiddaw Little Man. Skiddaw's main summit has grand views west, north and east but for a view to the south, Little Man is the place. Keswick and Derwent Water lie below and beyond them Borrowdale runs south towards Scafell Pike.

Summit of Helvellyn

Helvellyn has everything except a peaked summit; instead it has a broad plateau with a variety of cairns and this solid shelter, which can come in very handy on the wilder days. There's a glimpse of Windermere in the distance, with Morecambe Bay beyond.

Great Gable

I took this shot of Gable from Seathwaite Fell; I was pretty sure that sooner or later a shaft of sunlight would strike its flanks, and in fact I didn't have to wait too long. The eastern edge of the Napes crags can be seen near the centre of the shot.

Grains Gill and Borrowdale

I happened to glance back on my way up Grains Gill and was struck by the way the slopes framed the view down into Borrowdale and on towards Derwent Water and Skiddaw. The hill on the left is High Spy and on the right is Hind Crag.

Summit of Whiteless Pike

Ascending Whiteless Pike first makes a steep start to the day, but leads to the enticing ridge of Whiteless Edge. The summit of Wandope is on the right and the vast flank of Grasmoor on the left.

Carrock Mine and Brandy Gill
The notion that the Lakeland Fells are wild or unspoiled doesn't entirely stack up; many of them bear the marks of mining and quarrying. There are several notable mines in the northern fells, including Carrock Mine. The hill beyond is Bowscale Fell.

Browney Gill

Browney Gill is one of the feeders of Oxendale, at the head of Great Langdale. The gill itself can be followed by a fairly easy scramble, but this shot was taken from the popular path just above, which leads to Red Tarn, Pike o'Blisco and Crinkle Crags.

Moss and lichen
I liked the feeling of a miniature forest here, and also the way that the frost had persisted in the shadows.

Opposite: **The Scafell range from Grey Friar**
Grey Friar is the least-visited of the main Coniston tops; it lies on the 'wrong' side for anyone starting – as most people do – from Coniston. However it's well worth the detour for its unsurpassed views towards the Scafell range. The curious name may relate to a rock near the summit (not in this picture) which in certain lights bears a strong resemblance to a monk's hood.

Crinkle Crags from Pike o'Stickle
The light was rather fickle on this day, but it did briefly strike the slopes of Crinkle Crags at a perfect angle.

Opposite: **Kirk Fell and Pillar**
This shot was taken earlier on the same evening as the one on p41. The sun was hidden behind Kirk Fell, which brought the contrast level down and meant it was possible to capture the gradation of tones which made the more distant ridges seem translucent and unreal.

Pool on Souther Fell

It was a generally cloudy day and I wasn't finding a lot of inspiration, but I thought the shape of this pool had potential. The clouds parted sufficiently to give a gleam of light and – almost – reveal the top of Blencathra. The nearer fell is Bannerdale Crags.

Lord's Seat, Whitbarrow

The limestone ridges in the south-east part of the National Park may not be everyone's idea of fellwalking country, but they're too good to ignore. Whitbarrow is the biggest and the best. Lord's Seat is the highest point, but the full ridge – over 4 kilometres in length – should not be missed.

Scafell Crag

Scafell Crag is one of the finest – many would say *the* finest – of the Lakeland crags, but on a damp and misty day it's hardly surprising there were no climbers to be seen. There was, however, a party descending Broad Stand (in the lower left corner). This is a notorious place and I was concerned to see that one of the group appeared to be lowering the others without any form of belay. However, by the time I got nearer they'd all made it down safely.

Heather and oak wood, Rigg Beck

It was the contrast of colours that drew me to this scene. The stand of oaks on the fellside is now unusual but there would once have been many more like it. The present bare appearance of the fells is not natural, but results from millennia of clearance and grazing.

Blengdale from Little Gowder Crag
While I appreciated the pattern of becks and pools below me in Blengdale, I was also a little concerned to see how boggy it was, as it lay on my homeward route. In the end I decided not to attempt a short-cut across the valley floor but to take the longer, drier route around its head.

Opposite: **Causey Pike and Derwent Water**
Causey Pike is one of the most distinctive fells, its knobbly summit ridge identifiable from most angles.

Mickleden and Pike o'Stickle

Mickleden is one of the two subsidiary valleys at the head of Great Langdale, and one of the best examples of glacial action in the Lake District. Its textbook U-shape shows up well from this angle and so do the moraines (heaps of debris left by the retreating glacier) in the foreground.

Scafell Pike and Great Gable from High Spy

High Spy is one of the most evocative names in the District, and it certainly has some excellent views. The top is quite broad, however, and I needed to move around a fair bit during the evening to give depth to the views.

Little Langdale from Wet Side Edge

We'd spent several hours in thick cloud so when we finally dropped down into clearer air it was quite a revelation. A hint of sunlight around Little Langdale Tarn added an extra dimension. The nearer tarn is Greenburn Tarn.

Tarn Beck

Tarn Beck is a tributary of the Duddon and makes a great approach to Seathwaite Tarn and Grey Friar. For the scrambler this area is hard to beat: all three of the crags in shot have scrambling routes and so does the (hidden) continuation of the beck itself.

Ruddy Gill and Great End
Ruddy Gill is the main feeder of Grains Gill. If there's such a thing as a typical upland beck, this is a good candidate.

Great Stickle
This shot was taken above the Lickle valley, near Broughton Mills, on the south-west fringe of the fell country.

On the slopes of Seatallan

Seatallan is generally perceived as a broad grassy fell of little significance, but the wandering photographer can find a fair amount of rock on its slopes. The dark ridge in the middle distance is Yewbarrow and along the skyline are Kirk Fell, Great Gable, Scafell Pike and Scafell.

Opposite: **Above Striding Edge**

I'd made an early start as I wanted to get some pictures of Striding Edge without people. The weather was more cloudy than I'd hoped but the light was pretty dramatic at times – and I did get my unpopulated shots.

Great Carrs

I liked the gloomily dramatic mood of this view towards the Scafell range, but it needed something extra; I think the tiny figures of the walkers on the summit of Great Carrs give the necessary sense of scale.

Walker, Wandope Moss
This was a day of constantly changing weather and light; thick cloud, brilliant sunshine, flurries of snow. This shot has elements of all three. The lake below is Buttermere and the peak beyond is High Crag.

The Scafell range from Stonesty Pike

Stonesty Pike is a name that does not appear on most lists of fells, and I suppose it is nothing more than a trivial rise on the south ridge of Crinkle Crags. But it makes a great destination for anyone who wants to escape the crowds and enjoy the view over upper Eskdale in solitude.

Opposite: **Hindscarth and Robinson**

The Newlands valley is only a few miles from Keswick but fortunately has no 'attractions', and retains its peaceful atmosphere. It is almost completely surrounded by rugged fells and Hindscarth and Robinson have pride of place at the valley head.

Walkers near Blackbeck Tarn

It was a fine but typically hazy summer day, and I knew that long views would look very flat, so I lounged in the heather and waited for some walkers to appear in the right place. This is the approach to the much-loved little fell of Haystacks; the more distant slopes belong to High Crag and High Stile.

Middle Fell and Seatallan

On my last two visits to the western Wasdale fells – both long days – I've seen a grand total of two other walkers. Being able to go midweek and in the 'off' season certainly helps, but you'd still be highly unlikely to find such complete solitude in most other parts of the Lakes.

Falcon Crags, evening
Falcon Crags are the most spectacular of a line of crags which overlook the eastern shore of Derwent Water. Beyond the lake is Borrowdale and on the skyline, Scafell Pike and Great Gable.

Windermere from Gummer's How

Gummer's How stands above the lower end of Windermere and its combination of easy access and fine views makes it very popular. I descended a little to the north from the summit to find these larch trees framing the view.

The Ill Bell ridge from Harter Fell

Ill Bell (originally called Hill Bell) is the central peak of this triptych and it does indeed show a distinctive bell-like shape from almost any angle. Its supporting peaks are Yoke – on the left – and Froswick.

Walkers arriving at the summit of Blencathra

The most celebrated way to the top of Blencathra is by Sharp Edge, but the ridge of Hall's Fell is more continuous and leads directly to the summit. On this occasion there were numerous icy patches and the ascent had felt quite adventurous. The lake glinting in the distance is Thirlmere.

Glaramara and the Langdale Pikes from Whiteless Pike

A long lens helps to compress the distance between the ridges in this shot. The Langdale Pikes are seen from an unfamiliar angle; Pike o'Stickle is the prominent little cone in the centre and Harrison Stickle the blocky rise further left. The darker ridge forming the skyline further right is Glaramara.

Opposite: **The Duddon valley from Caw**

Size isn't everything, and though Caw is only 529 metres high, it's as rough and steep as almost any fell in the district. Its steepness gives great depth to the views all round, especially looking over the Duddon valley to the Scafell range.

Walkers descending from Catbells
Descending towards the Newlands valley from Catbells, the sun shone through briefly – just long enough for me to catch these other walkers. The prominent peak on the skyline is Causey Pike.

Opposite: **Dow Crag and the Isle of Man**
After a climb on Dow Crag, and a walk over the tops, we found ourselves on the summit of Coniston Old Man at sunset. It's difficult to know who was luckier, us or that lone figure on the summit of Dow Crag.

Skiddaw, Blencathra and Causey Pike

Compare this shot to the one on p89. This was taken an hour or so later, after we'd had breakfast. The last remnants of the mist soon cleared and a fine day followed, but it all seemed pretty ordinary after those early hours.

Skiddaw from Swirral Edge
Walkers on the main Helvellyn ridge and on the flanks of White Side help to suggest the scale in this shot. The distant hills on the left are in Scotland.

Overleaf: **Walker on Watson's Dodd**
For me, part of the appeal of the Lake District is the fact that it is a compact area; a strong walker can cross it in a day and many views give the impression of taking in the entire district. This isn't exactly true here (it rarely is) but that skyline does include many of the fells which have featured so often in this book: Bowfell, Crinkle Crags, Esk Pike, Scafell Pike, Great Gable, Kirk Fell and Pillar.